50 Premium American Diner Food

By: Kelly Johnson

Table of Contents

- Classic Bacon Cheeseburger
- Chicken Fried Steak
- Buttermilk Pancakes
- Meatloaf with Mashed Potatoes
- Chicken and Waffles
- Macaroni and Cheese
- BLT Sandwich
- Corned Beef Hash
- Buffalo Wings
- Shrimp and Grits
- Grilled Cheese and Tomato Soup
- Hot Roast Beef Sandwich
- Chicken Pot Pie
- Classic Reuben Sandwich
- Tuna Salad Sandwich
- French Toast with Maple Syrup
- Fish and Chips
- Philly Cheesesteak
- Grilled Tuna Melt
- Fried Green Tomatoes
- Sloppy Joes
- Pot Roast with Carrots and Potatoes
- Club Sandwich
- Classic Caesar Salad
- Sausage and Peppers
- Egg Salad Sandwich
- Diner-style Meatball Sub
- Breakfast Burrito
- Fried Chicken Sandwich
- Hot Dog with Onion Rings
- Steak and Eggs
- Beef Tacos
- Biscuits and Gravy
- Grilled Ham and Cheese
- Chili Con Carne

- Open-faced Turkey Sandwich
- Sweet Potato Fries
- Creamed Spinach
- Chicken Caesar Wrap
- Cheeseburger Sliders
- Pork Tenderloin Sandwich
- Nachos with Jalapeños
- Clam Chowder
- Tater Tots with Ketchup
- Country Fried Chicken
- Chicken Caesar Salad
- Southern Biscuits with Sausage Gravy
- Classic Cobb Salad
- BBQ Pulled Pork Sandwich
- Loaded Potato Skins

Classic Bacon Cheeseburger

Ingredients:

- 1 lb ground beef (80/20)
- 4 burger buns
- 4 slices cheddar cheese
- 4 strips of bacon, cooked
- Lettuce, tomato, pickles
- Ketchup, mustard, mayonnaise
- Salt and pepper to taste

Instructions:

1. Form the ground beef into 4 equal patties. Season with salt and pepper.
2. Grill or pan-fry the patties over medium heat for about 4-5 minutes per side, until cooked through.
3. Place a slice of cheese on each patty during the last minute of cooking to melt.
4. Toast the buns lightly.
5. Assemble the burgers with lettuce, tomato, pickle, and the cooked bacon. Add ketchup, mustard, and mayo if desired.
6. Serve with your favorite side.

Chicken Fried Steak

Ingredients:

- 4 beef steaks (tenderized)
- 1 cup all-purpose flour
- 1 tsp garlic powder
- 1 tsp onion powder
- 1 tsp paprika
- 1 tsp black pepper
- 1 tsp salt
- 2 eggs, beaten
- 1 cup buttermilk
- Vegetable oil for frying

Instructions:

1. Season the steaks with salt, pepper, garlic powder, onion powder, and paprika.
2. In one bowl, combine flour with seasoning. In another bowl, mix buttermilk and eggs.
3. Dredge the steaks in the flour mixture, then dip in the buttermilk, and coat again with flour.
4. Heat oil in a pan and fry steaks until golden brown on both sides, about 4 minutes per side.
5. Drain on paper towels and serve with white gravy.

Buttermilk Pancakes

Ingredients:

- 1 1/2 cups all-purpose flour
- 2 tbsp sugar
- 2 tsp baking powder
- 1/2 tsp baking soda
- 1/2 tsp salt
- 1 1/4 cups buttermilk
- 1 egg
- 2 tbsp melted butter
- Maple syrup for serving

Instructions:

1. In a large bowl, whisk together the dry ingredients.
2. In another bowl, whisk the wet ingredients.
3. Pour the wet ingredients into the dry and stir until just combined (lumps are fine).
4. Heat a non-stick skillet over medium heat and lightly grease.
5. Pour 1/4 cup batter onto the skillet for each pancake. Cook for 2-3 minutes per side, until golden.
6. Serve with maple syrup.

Meatloaf with Mashed Potatoes

Ingredients for Meatloaf:

- 1 lb ground beef
- 1 egg
- 1/2 cup breadcrumbs
- 1/4 cup milk
- 1/4 cup ketchup
- 1 tbsp Worcestershire sauce
- 1/2 tsp salt
- 1/2 tsp black pepper
- 1/2 tsp garlic powder
- 1/2 tsp onion powder

Ingredients for Mashed Potatoes:

- 2 lbs potatoes, peeled and cubed
- 1/4 cup milk
- 1/4 cup butter
- Salt and pepper to taste

Instructions:

1. Preheat the oven to 350°F (175°C).
2. Mix ground beef, egg, breadcrumbs, milk, ketchup, Worcestershire sauce, salt, pepper, garlic, and onion powder in a bowl.
3. Form the mixture into a loaf and place on a baking sheet.
4. Bake for 45 minutes to 1 hour.
5. Meanwhile, boil the potatoes in salted water until tender, then drain.
6. Mash the potatoes with milk, butter, salt, and pepper until smooth.
7. Serve the meatloaf with mashed potatoes.

Chicken and Waffles

Ingredients:

- 4 chicken tenders or chicken breasts, battered and fried
- 4 waffles, cooked
- Maple syrup
- Butter

Instructions:

1. Fry or bake chicken tenders or chicken breasts until crispy and cooked through.
2. Toast or make waffles and keep warm.
3. Serve the chicken on top of the waffles, drizzling with maple syrup and butter.

Macaroni and Cheese

Ingredients:

- 8 oz elbow macaroni
- 2 tbsp butter
- 2 tbsp flour
- 2 cups milk
- 2 cups shredded cheddar cheese
- Salt and pepper to taste

Instructions:

1. Cook the macaroni according to package directions and drain.
2. In a saucepan, melt butter over medium heat, then whisk in the flour. Cook for 1 minute.
3. Slowly add milk, whisking constantly, and cook until the sauce thickens.
4. Stir in the cheese until melted and smooth. Season with salt and pepper.
5. Toss the cheese sauce with the cooked macaroni and serve.

BLT Sandwich

Ingredients:

- 2 slices of bread, toasted
- 4 slices of bacon, cooked
- Lettuce
- Tomato slices
- Mayonnaise

Instructions:

1. Spread mayonnaise on each slice of toasted bread.
2. Layer with bacon, lettuce, and tomato slices.
3. Serve immediately.

Corned Beef Hash

Ingredients:

- 2 cups corned beef, chopped
- 1 medium onion, diced
- 2 cups diced potatoes (boiled or leftover)
- 1 tbsp vegetable oil
- Salt and pepper to taste
- 2 eggs (optional)

Instructions:

1. Heat oil in a skillet and sauté the onions until soft.
2. Add corned beef and potatoes, cooking until browned and crispy.
3. Season with salt and pepper.
4. Top with a fried egg if desired and serve.

Buffalo Wings

Ingredients:

- 12 chicken wings
- 1/4 cup butter, melted
- 1/4 cup hot sauce (like Frank's RedHot)
- Salt and pepper to taste
- Celery sticks
- Blue cheese dressing for dipping

Instructions:

1. Preheat oven to 400°F (200°C).
2. Season the wings with salt and pepper and bake for 25-30 minutes, turning halfway through.
3. In a bowl, mix melted butter and hot sauce.
4. Toss the cooked wings in the sauce mixture.
5. Serve with celery and blue cheese dressing.

Shrimp and Grits

Ingredients:

- 1 lb shrimp, peeled and deveined
- 1 cup grits
- 4 cups water or chicken broth
- 4 tbsp butter
- 1/2 cup heavy cream
- 1/4 cup cheddar cheese, shredded
- 2 cloves garlic, minced
- 1/2 tsp smoked paprika
- Salt and pepper to taste
- Chopped green onions for garnish

Instructions:

1. Cook the grits according to the package directions, using water or chicken broth. Stir in butter, cream, and cheddar cheese. Keep warm.
2. In a skillet, sauté the garlic in a little butter until fragrant. Add the shrimp, paprika, salt, and pepper. Cook until the shrimp are pink and cooked through, about 3-4 minutes.
3. Serve the shrimp over the creamy grits and garnish with green onions.

Grilled Cheese and Tomato Soup

Ingredients for Grilled Cheese:

- 2 slices of bread
- 2 tbsp butter
- 2 slices of cheddar cheese

Ingredients for Tomato Soup:

- 1 can (14 oz) crushed tomatoes
- 1/2 cup onion, diced
- 1 clove garlic, minced
- 2 cups chicken broth
- 1/4 cup heavy cream
- 1 tbsp olive oil
- Salt and pepper to taste

Instructions:

1. **For the Soup:** Heat olive oil in a pot and sauté the onion and garlic until soft. Add the crushed tomatoes, chicken broth, salt, and pepper. Simmer for 15 minutes.
2. Stir in heavy cream and blend the soup until smooth using an immersion blender or regular blender.
3. **For the Grilled Cheese:** Butter the outside of each slice of bread and place cheese between the slices. Grill in a skillet over medium heat until golden brown on both sides.
4. Serve the grilled cheese with the tomato soup.

Hot Roast Beef Sandwich

Ingredients:

- 1 lb roast beef, thinly sliced
- 2 sandwich rolls or baguette
- 1/2 cup beef gravy
- 1/4 cup mustard or horseradish sauce (optional)
- Sliced pickles for garnish

Instructions:

1. Heat the beef slices in a pan with a little bit of gravy to warm them up.
2. Split the rolls or baguette and toast lightly if desired.
3. Pile the warm beef onto the sandwich rolls, spoon over extra gravy, and top with mustard or horseradish sauce. Garnish with pickles.
4. Serve immediately.

Chicken Pot Pie

Ingredients for Filling:

- 2 cups cooked chicken, diced
- 1 cup frozen peas and carrots
- 1/2 cup onion, diced
- 1/4 cup butter
- 1/4 cup flour
- 2 cups chicken broth
- 1 cup heavy cream
- Salt and pepper to taste

Ingredients for Crust:

- 1 package refrigerated pie crusts (or homemade)

Instructions:

1. Preheat the oven to 400°F (200°C).
2. In a saucepan, melt butter and sauté onions until soft. Stir in the flour and cook for 1 minute.
3. Gradually add chicken broth and cream, stirring until thickened. Add the chicken, peas, carrots, salt, and pepper.
4. Place one pie crust in a baking dish, pour the filling inside, and cover with the second pie crust. Seal the edges and cut slits in the top crust.
5. Bake for 30-40 minutes, until golden brown.

Classic Reuben Sandwich

Ingredients:

- 2 slices of rye bread
- 4 oz corned beef, sliced
- 2 slices Swiss cheese
- 2 tbsp sauerkraut
- 2 tbsp Russian or Thousand Island dressing
- Butter for grilling

Instructions:

1. Spread dressing on the inside of both slices of bread.
2. Layer one slice of bread with corned beef, Swiss cheese, and sauerkraut.
3. Top with the second slice of bread, butter the outside of the sandwich, and grill in a skillet until golden brown on both sides.
4. Serve immediately.

Tuna Salad Sandwich

Ingredients:

- 1 can tuna, drained
- 2 tbsp mayonnaise
- 1 tbsp Dijon mustard
- 1/4 cup celery, finely chopped
- 1/4 cup red onion, finely chopped
- Salt and pepper to taste
- 2 slices of bread or a sandwich roll

Instructions:

1. In a bowl, combine tuna, mayonnaise, mustard, celery, onion, salt, and pepper.
2. Spread the tuna mixture on a slice of bread or sandwich roll.
3. Top with another slice of bread and serve.

French Toast with Maple Syrup

Ingredients:

- 4 slices of bread (preferably a thick variety like brioche or challah)
- 2 eggs
- 1/2 cup milk
- 1 tsp cinnamon
- 1/2 tsp vanilla extract
- Butter for frying
- Maple syrup for serving

Instructions:

1. In a bowl, whisk together eggs, milk, cinnamon, and vanilla extract.
2. Dip each slice of bread into the egg mixture, coating both sides.
3. Heat a skillet over medium heat and melt a little butter. Fry the bread on both sides until golden brown.
4. Serve with maple syrup.

Fish and Chips

Ingredients:

- 4 white fish fillets (like cod or haddock)
- 1 cup all-purpose flour
- 1 tsp baking powder
- 1/2 tsp salt
- 1/2 tsp pepper
- 1 cup cold beer or sparkling water
- 1 lb potatoes, peeled and cut into fries
- Oil for frying

Instructions:

1. Heat oil in a deep fryer or large pot to 350°F (175°C).
2. For the batter, mix flour, baking powder, salt, and pepper in a bowl. Gradually add the cold beer or sparkling water until you have a smooth batter.
3. Dip fish fillets into the batter and fry for 4-5 minutes until crispy and golden brown.
4. Fry the potatoes in the same oil until golden and crispy.
5. Serve the fish and chips with malt vinegar or tartar sauce.

Philly Cheesesteak

Ingredients:

- 1 lb thinly sliced rib-eye steak
- 2 tbsp olive oil
- 1 onion, sliced
- 2 bell peppers, sliced
- 4 hoagie rolls
- 8 slices provolone cheese
- Salt and pepper to taste

Instructions:

1. Heat olive oil in a pan and sauté the onions and bell peppers until softened.
2. Season the steak with salt and pepper, and add it to the pan, cooking until browned and cooked through.
3. Toast the hoagie rolls, and then layer with the steak, vegetables, and slices of provolone cheese.
4. Serve hot.

Grilled Tuna Melt

Ingredients:

- 1 can tuna, drained and flaked
- 2 tbsp mayonnaise
- 1 tbsp Dijon mustard
- 1/4 cup red onion, finely chopped
- 4 slices bread (sourdough or whole wheat)
- 4 slices Swiss or cheddar cheese
- Butter for grilling

Instructions:

1. In a bowl, combine tuna, mayonnaise, mustard, and red onion. Stir until well mixed.
2. Spread the tuna mixture evenly on two slices of bread. Top with cheese and cover with the remaining bread slices.
3. Butter the outside of each sandwich and grill in a skillet over medium heat until both sides are golden brown and the cheese is melted, about 3-4 minutes per side.
4. Serve hot.

Fried Green Tomatoes

Ingredients:

- 4 medium green tomatoes, sliced into 1/2-inch thick slices
- 1 cup cornmeal
- 1/2 cup all-purpose flour
- 1 tsp salt
- 1/2 tsp black pepper
- 1/2 tsp cayenne pepper (optional)
- 1 cup buttermilk
- Oil for frying

Instructions:

1. Mix the cornmeal, flour, salt, pepper, and cayenne (if using) in a shallow bowl.
2. Dip the tomato slices into the buttermilk, then dredge in the cornmeal mixture to coat evenly.
3. Heat oil in a frying pan over medium-high heat. Fry the tomato slices in batches for 2-3 minutes per side until crispy and golden.
4. Drain on paper towels and serve hot.

Sloppy Joes

Ingredients:

- 1 lb ground beef
- 1 small onion, diced
- 1 bell pepper, diced
- 2 cloves garlic, minced
- 1 cup tomato sauce
- 2 tbsp tomato paste
- 2 tbsp Worcestershire sauce
- 2 tbsp ketchup
- 1 tbsp mustard
- 1/2 tsp paprika
- Salt and pepper to taste
- 4 hamburger buns

Instructions:

1. In a skillet, cook the ground beef over medium heat until browned. Drain excess fat.
2. Add the onion, bell pepper, and garlic. Cook for 3-4 minutes until softened.
3. Stir in tomato sauce, tomato paste, Worcestershire sauce, ketchup, mustard, paprika, salt, and pepper. Simmer for 10-15 minutes, until the mixture thickens.
4. Spoon the sloppy joe mixture onto the bottom half of the buns and top with the other half. Serve immediately.

Pot Roast with Carrots and Potatoes

Ingredients:

- 3-4 lb beef chuck roast
- 1 tbsp olive oil
- 1 onion, quartered
- 3 cloves garlic, smashed
- 4 carrots, peeled and cut into chunks
- 4 potatoes, peeled and cut into chunks
- 1 cup beef broth
- 1 cup red wine (optional)
- 1 tsp dried thyme
- Salt and pepper to taste

Instructions:

1. Preheat the oven to 350°F (175°C).
2. Heat olive oil in a large Dutch oven over medium-high heat. Brown the roast on all sides, about 4-5 minutes per side. Remove the roast and set aside.
3. Add onion and garlic to the pot and sauté for 2-3 minutes. Add beef broth, red wine (if using), thyme, salt, and pepper.
4. Return the roast to the pot and add the carrots and potatoes around the roast.
5. Cover and cook in the oven for 3-4 hours, or until the meat is tender and easily pulls apart.
6. Serve with the vegetables and pan juices.

Club Sandwich

Ingredients:

- 6 slices of bread (white or whole wheat)
- 6 oz deli turkey or chicken
- 4 slices crispy bacon
- 2 slices Swiss or cheddar cheese
- 1/4 cup mayonnaise
- Lettuce
- Tomato slices
- Salt and pepper to taste

Instructions:

1. Toast the bread slices and spread mayonnaise on each slice.
2. Layer the sandwich: Start with a slice of bread, then add turkey, cheese, lettuce, and tomato. Add another slice of bread, and layer with bacon, more turkey, and cheese. Top with the final slice of bread.
3. Cut the sandwich into quarters and serve with chips or pickles.

Classic Caesar Salad

Ingredients for the Dressing:

- 1/4 cup mayonnaise
- 1/4 cup grated Parmesan cheese
- 2 tbsp lemon juice
- 1 clove garlic, minced
- 1 tsp Dijon mustard
- 1 tsp Worcestershire sauce
- Salt and pepper to taste

Ingredients for the Salad:

- 4 cups romaine lettuce, chopped
- 1 cup croutons
- 1/4 cup grated Parmesan cheese

Instructions:

1. To make the dressing, whisk together mayonnaise, Parmesan, lemon juice, garlic, mustard, Worcestershire sauce, salt, and pepper.
2. Toss the lettuce with the dressing, croutons, and Parmesan cheese.
3. Serve immediately as a side salad.

Sausage and Peppers

Ingredients:

- 4 Italian sausages (sweet or spicy)
- 1 onion, sliced
- 2 bell peppers, sliced
- 2 cloves garlic, minced
- 1/2 tsp red pepper flakes (optional)
- 1 tbsp olive oil
- Salt and pepper to taste

Instructions:

1. Heat olive oil in a skillet over medium-high heat. Brown the sausages, turning occasionally, until cooked through (about 10-12 minutes). Remove and set aside.
2. In the same skillet, add onion, bell peppers, garlic, and red pepper flakes. Sauté for 5-7 minutes until softened.
3. Slice the sausages and add them back to the skillet. Cook for an additional 5 minutes.
4. Serve with crusty bread or over pasta.

Egg Salad Sandwich

Ingredients:

- 6 hard-boiled eggs, chopped
- 1/4 cup mayonnaise
- 1 tbsp Dijon mustard
- 1 tbsp pickle relish (optional)
- Salt and pepper to taste
- 2 slices of bread

Instructions:

1. In a bowl, combine chopped eggs, mayonnaise, mustard, relish (if using), salt, and pepper.
2. Spread the egg salad on a slice of bread and top with the other slice.
3. Serve immediately.

Diner-style Meatball Sub

Ingredients:

- 1 lb ground beef
- 1/4 cup breadcrumbs
- 1/4 cup grated Parmesan cheese
- 1 egg
- 1 tsp garlic powder
- 1 tsp dried oregano
- Salt and pepper to taste
- 2 cups marinara sauce
- 4 sub rolls
- 4 slices provolone cheese

Instructions:

1. Preheat the oven to 375°F (190°C).
2. In a bowl, combine ground beef, breadcrumbs, Parmesan, egg, garlic powder, oregano, salt, and pepper. Form into meatballs (about 12).
3. Brown the meatballs in a skillet over medium heat, then add marinara sauce. Simmer for 10-15 minutes.
4. Split the sub rolls and place a meatball and some sauce in each roll. Top with a slice of provolone cheese.
5. Place in the oven for 5-7 minutes to melt the cheese.
6. Serve hot.

Breakfast Burrito

Ingredients:

- 4 large flour tortillas
- 6 eggs, scrambled
- 1 cup cooked breakfast sausage, crumbled
- 1/2 cup shredded cheddar cheese
- 1/4 cup salsa
- 1/4 cup sour cream (optional)
- 1/2 avocado, sliced (optional)
- Salt and pepper to taste

Instructions:

1. Scramble the eggs in a skillet over medium heat. Season with salt and pepper.
2. In another pan, cook the breakfast sausage until browned, then crumble it.
3. Warm the tortillas in a dry skillet or microwave.
4. To assemble, layer scrambled eggs, sausage, shredded cheese, salsa, and avocado (if using) onto each tortilla.
5. Roll up the tortillas, folding in the sides as you go.
6. Serve with a side of sour cream and extra salsa if desired.

Fried Chicken Sandwich

Ingredients:

- 2 boneless chicken breasts
- 1 cup buttermilk
- 1 cup all-purpose flour
- 1 tsp paprika
- 1 tsp garlic powder
- 1/2 tsp salt
- 1/2 tsp pepper
- Vegetable oil for frying
- 4 sandwich buns
- Lettuce and tomato slices
- Mayonnaise or hot sauce (optional)

Instructions:

1. Marinate the chicken breasts in buttermilk for at least 1 hour.
2. In a shallow bowl, combine flour, paprika, garlic powder, salt, and pepper.
3. Heat oil in a large skillet over medium-high heat.
4. Dredge the marinated chicken in the flour mixture and fry for 6-7 minutes per side until golden and crispy.
5. Toast the buns and assemble the sandwich by placing the fried chicken on the bottom bun. Top with lettuce, tomato, and mayonnaise or hot sauce.
6. Serve hot.

Hot Dog with Onion Rings

Ingredients:

- 4 hot dog buns
- 4 beef hot dogs
- 1 large onion, sliced into rings
- 1 cup buttermilk
- 1 cup all-purpose flour
- 1 tsp paprika
- 1/2 tsp garlic powder
- Salt and pepper to taste
- Vegetable oil for frying

Instructions:

1. Heat the hot dogs in boiling water or grill them until heated through.
2. For the onion rings, dip the onion slices into buttermilk, then coat with a mixture of flour, paprika, garlic powder, salt, and pepper.
3. Heat oil in a skillet or deep fryer to 375°F (190°C).
4. Fry the onion rings for 2-3 minutes until golden brown and crispy. Drain on paper towels.
5. Assemble the hot dogs in buns and top with fried onion rings.
6. Serve with ketchup and mustard if desired.

Steak and Eggs

Ingredients:

- 2 steaks (ribeye, sirloin, or your choice)
- 4 eggs
- 2 tbsp olive oil
- 1 tbsp butter
- Salt and pepper to taste
- Fresh parsley for garnish (optional)

Instructions:

1. Season the steaks with salt and pepper. Heat olive oil in a skillet over medium-high heat.
2. Cook the steaks to your desired level of doneness, about 4-5 minutes per side for medium-rare. Remove and let rest.
3. In the same skillet, melt butter and crack in the eggs. Cook until the whites are set but the yolks are still runny (or cook longer for hard eggs).
4. Serve the steaks with eggs on the side, garnished with fresh parsley if desired.

Beef Tacos

Ingredients:

- 1 lb ground beef
- 1 packet taco seasoning
- 1/2 cup water
- 8 small taco shells
- Shredded lettuce
- Diced tomatoes
- Shredded cheese
- Salsa
- Sour cream (optional)

Instructions:

1. Brown the ground beef in a skillet over medium heat. Drain excess fat.
2. Stir in taco seasoning and water. Simmer for 5-7 minutes until the sauce thickens.
3. Warm the taco shells according to package instructions.
4. To assemble, spoon the beef mixture into each taco shell, then top with lettuce, tomatoes, cheese, salsa, and sour cream.
5. Serve with extra salsa and lime wedges if desired.

Biscuits and Gravy

Ingredients for the Biscuits:

- 2 cups all-purpose flour
- 2 tsp baking powder
- 1/2 tsp salt
- 1/2 cup cold butter, cubed
- 3/4 cup milk

Ingredients for the Gravy:

- 1 lb breakfast sausage
- 2 tbsp all-purpose flour
- 2 cups milk
- Salt and pepper to taste

Instructions:

1. Preheat the oven to 425°F (220°C).
2. For the biscuits, combine flour, baking powder, and salt. Cut in the cold butter until the mixture resembles coarse crumbs.
3. Stir in the milk to form a dough. Roll out on a floured surface and cut into biscuits.
4. Place the biscuits on a baking sheet and bake for 12-15 minutes until golden.
5. For the gravy, brown the sausage in a skillet over medium heat. Add flour and cook for 1-2 minutes.
6. Stir in milk and simmer until the gravy thickens. Season with salt and pepper.
7. Serve the biscuits topped with gravy.

Grilled Ham and Cheese

Ingredients:

- 4 slices of bread
- 4 slices of ham
- 4 slices of cheese (Swiss, cheddar, or your choice)
- Butter for grilling

Instructions:

1. Butter one side of each slice of bread.
2. Layer ham and cheese between the unbuttered sides of the bread slices.
3. Heat a skillet over medium heat. Grill the sandwiches, butter side down, for 3-4 minutes per side until golden brown and the cheese is melted.
4. Serve hot.

Chili Con Carne

Ingredients:

- 1 lb ground beef
- 1 onion, chopped
- 2 cloves garlic, minced
- 1 can kidney beans, drained and rinsed
- 1 can diced tomatoes
- 1 tbsp chili powder
- 1 tsp cumin
- Salt and pepper to taste
- 1/2 cup beef broth

Instructions:

1. Brown the ground beef in a pot over medium heat. Drain any excess fat.
2. Add onion and garlic, and cook for 3-4 minutes until softened.
3. Stir in the beans, tomatoes, chili powder, cumin, salt, pepper, and beef broth.
4. Simmer for 20-30 minutes, stirring occasionally, until the chili thickens.
5. Serve hot, topped with cheese or sour cream if desired.

Open-faced Turkey Sandwich

Ingredients:

- 2 slices of bread
- 1 cup cooked turkey, shredded
- 1/2 cup gravy
- 1/4 cup cranberry sauce (optional)

Instructions:

1. Toast the bread slices and place them on a plate.
2. Heat the turkey and gravy in a skillet until warmed through.
3. Spoon the turkey and gravy mixture onto each slice of bread.
4. Top with cranberry sauce if desired, and serve.

Sweet Potato Fries

Ingredients:

- 2 large sweet potatoes, peeled and cut into fries
- 2 tbsp olive oil
- 1 tsp paprika
- 1/2 tsp garlic powder
- Salt and pepper to taste

Instructions:

1. Preheat the oven to 425°F (220°C).
2. Toss the sweet potato fries with olive oil, paprika, garlic powder, salt, and pepper.
3. Spread the fries in a single layer on a baking sheet.
4. Bake for 25-30 minutes, flipping halfway through, until crispy and golden.
5. Serve hot with ketchup or your favorite dipping sauce.

Creamed Spinach

Ingredients:

- 1 lb fresh spinach (or 2 packages frozen spinach, thawed and drained)
- 2 tbsp butter
- 1 small onion, finely chopped
- 2 cloves garlic, minced
- 1 cup heavy cream
- 1/2 cup grated Parmesan cheese
- Salt and pepper to taste
- Fresh nutmeg (optional)

Instructions:

1. If using fresh spinach, wilt it in a large pot over medium heat, then drain excess water. If using frozen spinach, squeeze out excess moisture.
2. In a large skillet, melt butter over medium heat. Add onion and garlic and sauté until softened, about 3-4 minutes.
3. Add the spinach and stir to combine. Pour in the heavy cream and bring to a simmer.
4. Stir in the Parmesan cheese, salt, pepper, and a pinch of nutmeg, if using. Simmer for 3-5 minutes until thickened.
5. Serve hot as a side dish.

Chicken Caesar Wrap

Ingredients:

- 2 large flour tortillas
- 2 grilled chicken breasts, sliced
- 1 cup Romaine lettuce, chopped
- 1/4 cup Caesar dressing
- 1/4 cup shredded Parmesan cheese
- 1/4 cup croutons, crushed (optional)

Instructions:

1. In a large bowl, toss the chicken, lettuce, Caesar dressing, and Parmesan cheese together.
2. Place the mixture evenly onto each tortilla.
3. Sprinkle with crushed croutons for added crunch, if desired.
4. Fold the sides of the tortilla and roll up tightly to form the wrap.
5. Serve immediately or wrap in foil for an on-the-go lunch.

Cheeseburger Sliders

Ingredients:

- 1 lb ground beef
- 1/2 tsp salt
- 1/4 tsp black pepper
- 12 slider buns
- 6 slices cheddar cheese, halved
- Ketchup and mustard (optional)
- Pickles (optional)
- Lettuce and tomato slices (optional)

Instructions:

1. Preheat your grill or skillet to medium-high heat.
2. Season the ground beef with salt and pepper, then form into 12 small patties.
3. Cook the patties for about 2-3 minutes per side until cooked through and browned.
4. During the last minute of cooking, place half a slice of cheese on each patty to melt.
5. Toast the slider buns on the grill or in the oven for 1-2 minutes.
6. Assemble the sliders by placing each cheeseburger patty on a bun and adding ketchup, mustard, pickles, lettuce, and tomato if desired.
7. Serve immediately.

Pork Tenderloin Sandwich

Ingredients:

- 1 pork tenderloin (about 1 lb)
- 1 tbsp olive oil
- Salt and pepper to taste
- 4 sandwich buns
- 1/4 cup mayonnaise
- 2 tbsp Dijon mustard
- 1/4 cup sliced pickles
- Lettuce and tomato slices

Instructions:

1. Preheat the oven to 375°F (190°C).
2. Season the pork tenderloin with salt, pepper, and olive oil. Roast in the oven for 20-25 minutes until the internal temperature reaches 145°F (63°C).
3. Allow the pork to rest for 10 minutes before slicing it thinly.
4. Mix mayonnaise and Dijon mustard in a small bowl.
5. Toast the sandwich buns and spread the mayonnaise mixture on each bun.
6. Layer the sliced pork on the buns, then top with pickles, lettuce, and tomato.
7. Serve immediately.

Nachos with Jalapeños

Ingredients:

- 1 bag tortilla chips
- 1 1/2 cups shredded cheddar cheese
- 1 1/2 cups shredded Monterey Jack cheese
- 1/2 cup sliced jalapeños (fresh or pickled)
- 1/2 cup sour cream
- 1/4 cup salsa
- 1/4 cup sliced green onions (optional)

Instructions:

1. Preheat the oven to 375°F (190°C).
2. Spread the tortilla chips in an even layer on a baking sheet.
3. Sprinkle the cheddar and Monterey Jack cheeses evenly over the chips.
4. Add jalapeño slices on top of the cheese.
5. Bake for 10-12 minutes, or until the cheese is melted and bubbly.
6. Remove from the oven and drizzle with sour cream and salsa.
7. Garnish with sliced green onions, if desired, and serve hot.

Clam Chowder

Ingredients:

- 2 tbsp butter
- 1 small onion, chopped
- 2 stalks celery, chopped
- 2 medium potatoes, peeled and diced
- 1 can (10 oz) clams, drained and chopped, with juice reserved
- 1 1/2 cups clam juice
- 2 cups heavy cream
- 1 tsp thyme
- Salt and pepper to taste
- Fresh parsley for garnish

Instructions:

1. In a large pot, melt butter over medium heat. Add the onion and celery and sauté for 4-5 minutes until softened.
2. Add the diced potatoes, clam juice, and reserved clam juice. Bring to a simmer and cook for 10-15 minutes until the potatoes are tender.
3. Stir in the clams and heavy cream. Simmer for an additional 5 minutes, then season with thyme, salt, and pepper.
4. Garnish with fresh parsley and serve hot.

Tater Tots with Ketchup

Ingredients:

- 1 package frozen tater tots
- Ketchup for dipping

Instructions:

1. Preheat the oven according to the instructions on the tater tots package.
2. Spread the tater tots on a baking sheet in a single layer.
3. Bake according to package instructions until golden and crispy, about 20-25 minutes.
4. Serve hot with ketchup for dipping.

Country Fried Chicken

Ingredients:

- 4 bone-in, skin-on chicken breasts
- 1 cup buttermilk
- 1 egg
- 1 1/2 cups all-purpose flour
- 1 tsp salt
- 1 tsp black pepper
- 1 tsp garlic powder
- 1 tsp paprika
- 1/2 tsp cayenne pepper (optional)
- Vegetable oil for frying

Instructions:

1. In a bowl, whisk together buttermilk and egg. Submerge the chicken breasts in the mixture and let it marinate for at least 30 minutes.
2. In a separate bowl, mix together flour, salt, pepper, garlic powder, paprika, and cayenne pepper.
3. Heat about 1 inch of vegetable oil in a large skillet over medium-high heat.
4. Dredge the marinated chicken in the flour mixture, pressing down lightly to coat evenly.
5. Fry the chicken in batches for about 6-8 minutes per side, or until golden brown and the internal temperature reaches 165°F (74°C).
6. Remove the chicken and drain on paper towels. Serve hot.

Chicken Caesar Salad

Ingredients:

- 2 grilled chicken breasts, sliced
- 4 cups Romaine lettuce, chopped
- 1/4 cup grated Parmesan cheese
- 1/2 cup Caesar dressing
- Croutons (optional)
- Fresh ground black pepper

Instructions:

1. In a large bowl, toss the chopped Romaine lettuce with Caesar dressing until well coated.
2. Add the sliced grilled chicken on top of the salad.
3. Sprinkle with grated Parmesan cheese and add croutons, if using.
4. Season with freshly ground black pepper to taste.
5. Serve immediately.

Southern Biscuits with Sausage Gravy

Ingredients:

For the Biscuits:

- 2 cups all-purpose flour
- 1 tbsp baking powder
- 1/2 tsp salt
- 1/2 cup cold unsalted butter, cubed
- 3/4 cup buttermilk

For the Sausage Gravy:

- 1 lb breakfast sausage
- 2 tbsp all-purpose flour
- 2 cups whole milk
- Salt and black pepper to taste

Instructions:

1. **For the Biscuits:** Preheat the oven to 450°F (232°C). In a bowl, combine the flour, baking powder, and salt. Cut in the butter using a pastry cutter or your hands until the mixture resembles coarse crumbs. Add the buttermilk and stir until just combined.
2. Turn the dough out onto a floured surface and gently knead it a few times. Pat it into a rectangle about 1 inch thick. Use a biscuit cutter to cut out biscuits and place them on a baking sheet.
3. Bake for 10-12 minutes until golden brown.
4. **For the Sausage Gravy:** While the biscuits bake, brown the sausage in a large skillet over medium heat, breaking it up as it cooks. Once the sausage is browned, sprinkle in the flour and cook for 1-2 minutes, stirring constantly.
5. Gradually add the milk, stirring until the gravy thickens. Season with salt and pepper.
6. Split the warm biscuits in half and pour the sausage gravy over the top. Serve immediately.

Classic Cobb Salad

Ingredients:

- 2 cups Romaine lettuce, chopped
- 2 cups mixed greens
- 2 cooked chicken breasts, diced
- 1 avocado, diced
- 1/2 cup cherry tomatoes, halved
- 1/4 cup crumbled blue cheese
- 2 hard-boiled eggs, sliced
- 4 slices cooked bacon, crumbled
- 1/4 cup red onion, thinly sliced
- 1/4 cup ranch or vinaigrette dressing

Instructions:

1. In a large bowl, toss the Romaine lettuce and mixed greens.
2. Arrange the diced chicken, avocado, cherry tomatoes, blue cheese, hard-boiled eggs, bacon, and red onion on top in sections.
3. Drizzle with your choice of dressing and serve immediately.

BBQ Pulled Pork Sandwich

Ingredients:

- 2 lbs pork shoulder (or butt)
- 1 tbsp olive oil
- Salt and pepper to taste
- 1 cup BBQ sauce
- 4 hamburger buns
- Coleslaw (optional)

Instructions:

1. Preheat the oven to 325°F (165°C). Rub the pork shoulder with olive oil, salt, and pepper.
2. Place the pork in a roasting pan and cover with aluminum foil. Roast for about 4 hours, or until the meat is tender and shreds easily.
3. Remove the pork from the oven and let it rest for 10 minutes. Use two forks to shred the meat.
4. Toss the shredded pork with BBQ sauce until well coated.
5. Pile the pulled pork onto the buns and top with coleslaw, if desired. Serve immediately.

Loaded Potato Skins

Ingredients:

- 4 large russet potatoes
- 2 tbsp olive oil
- Salt and pepper to taste
- 1/2 cup shredded cheddar cheese
- 1/4 cup sour cream
- 4 slices cooked bacon, crumbled
- 2 green onions, chopped
- 1/4 cup grated Parmesan cheese

Instructions:

1. Preheat the oven to 400°F (200°C). Wash and dry the potatoes. Rub them with olive oil and sprinkle with salt. Prick the potatoes with a fork and bake them for 45-60 minutes, until tender.
2. Once the potatoes are cool enough to handle, slice them in half and scoop out the flesh, leaving a small border around the edge.
3. Brush the skins with olive oil, season with salt and pepper, and return them to the oven. Bake for an additional 10 minutes until crispy.
4. Remove from the oven and fill each potato skin with shredded cheddar cheese, bacon crumbles, and Parmesan. Return to the oven for 5-7 minutes until the cheese is melted.
5. Top with sour cream and chopped green onions. Serve hot.

www.ingramcontent.com/pod-product-compliance
Lightning Source LLC
LaVergne TN
LVHW081343060526
838201LV00055B/2823